IELTS Writing Task 2 Vocabulary

100 High-Scoring Collocations You Need to Know

TheBrainstormingStation.com

VOCABULARY

WHAT ARE COLLOCATIONS?

Collocations are combinations of words that frequently appear together in English. These word pairs or phrases sound natural to native English speakers because they are commonly used in everyday language.

Collocations can consist of two or more words, such as verb-noun pairs, adjective-noun pairs, verb-adverb pairs, and adjective-adverb pairs.

Examples of collocations:

- Make a decision.
- Strong coffee.
- Highly recommend.
- Deeply rooted.

Why are collocations important?

Using collocations in your writing can improve the overall quality and fluency of your essay, which ultimately impacts your IELTS writing score. Here are some reasons why collocations are crucial for your writing:

Naturalness: Collocations make your writing sound more natural and native-like, increasing your lexical resource score.

Vocabulary Range: Employing a variety of collocations showcases your range of vocabulary and understanding of language patterns.

Coherence and Cohesion: Collocations can help you create more coherent and cohesive sentences, improving the flow of your essay.

How Collocations Impact Your Writing Score

Let's understand how using collocations can positively impact your IELTS Writing Task 2 score and contribute to achieving higher marks in each assessment criterion.

Collocations and Task Response:

Using appropriate collocations can make your arguments and ideas more convincing, thereby improving your task response. Additionally, accurate collocations can help you demonstrate a clear understanding of the question and convey your position more effectively.

Collocations and Coherence and Cohesion:

Collocations can improve the coherence and cohesion of your essay by creating natural-sounding connections between ideas. They enable you to express your thoughts more clearly and efficiently, allowing for a smoother flow of information.

Collocations and Lexical Resource:

Employing collocations in your writing demonstrates a wide range of vocabulary and familiarity with natural language patterns. By using varied and precise collocations, you can showcase your lexical resource and increase your chances of receiving a higher score in this criterion.

Collocations and Grammatical Range and Accuracy:

Collocations often adhere to specific grammatical patterns, making them an excellent tool for showcasing your grammatical range and accuracy. Utilizing collocations correctly can help you avoid common grammatical mistakes and produce sentences that are both structurally accurate and engaging.

Tips for Using Collocations Effectively

Learn collocations in context: When studying collocations, focus on understanding how they fit into sentences and paragraphs, rather than memorizing them in isolation.

Practice using collocations: Integrate collocations into your writing practice to build familiarity and confidence in using them effectively.

Read widely: Exposure to various texts, such as articles, essays, and books, can help you identify common collocations and understand how they are used in different contexts.

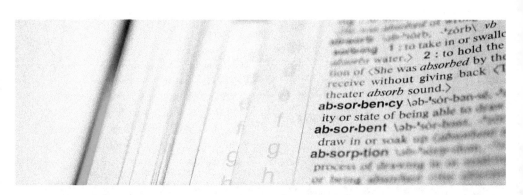

100 HIGH-SCORING COLLOCATIONS YOU NEED TO KNOW FOR IELTS WRITING TASK 2

In this section, we will review more high-scoring collocations and examples of how we can use them in sentences. Almost all of these collocations are academic collocations and therefore, you can use them in your IELTS Writing task 2 essays.

For each collocation, you will read 3 different example sentences. Reading multiple examples will give you the flexibility to use the collocations accurately and appropriately.

1.

To deal with, handle, or confront a particular matter or difficulty that needs attention or resolution.

To address the issue/problem

- In order to address the issue of unemployment, the government must invest more in education and skill development programs, thereby creating a highly skilled workforce that meets the demands of various industries.

- The new policy aims to address the problem of air pollution by imposing stricter regulations on vehicle emissions and promoting the use of renewable energy sources in transportation.

- To effectively address the issue of climate change, it is crucial for countries to collaborate on a global scale and adopt sustainable practices in agriculture, energy production, and waste management.

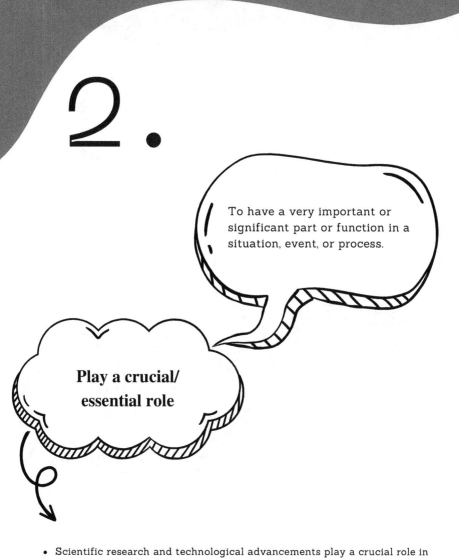

2.

> To have a very important or significant part or function in a situation, event, or process.

Play a crucial/ essential role

- Scientific research and technological advancements play a crucial role in addressing global challenges such as climate change, food security, and public health.

- Teachers play an essential role in shaping the minds of young students, providing not only academic knowledge but also instilling moral values and critical thinking skills.

- Parental involvement plays a crucial role in a child's academic success, as it fosters a supportive and nurturing environment that encourages learning and intellectual curiosity.

3.

To confront, attempt to solve, or deal with a difficult situation, challenge, or issue.

To tackle the problem

- In order to tackle the problem of obesity, public health campaigns should focus on promoting healthier lifestyles, including a balanced diet and regular exercise, while also addressing the socio-economic factors that contribute to this epidemic.

- The government has launched an ambitious plan to tackle the problem of drug addiction by providing better access to rehabilitation centers, funding research on innovative treatment methods, and enforcing stricter penalties for drug traffickers.

- To ackle the problem of income inequality, policymakers must consider implementing progressive tax systems and providing a comprehensive social safety net for vulnerable populations.

4.

A large variety or diverse assortment of items, ideas, or elements, often spanning across various categories or fields.

A wide range of

- Climate change has a wide range of consequences, including the loss of biodiversity, increased frequency of extreme weather events, and a decline in agricultural productivity.

- A wide range of factors contribute to the rising cost of healthcare, such as an aging population, advances in medical technology, and the prevalence of chronic diseases.

- The university offers a wide range of courses in various disciplines, enabling students to explore their interests and develop a well-rounded educational experience.

5.

A significant or pressing issue, worry, or challenge that requires attention, discussion, or action.

A major concern

- Water scarcity has become a major concern in many parts of the world, as climate change exacerbates existing problems related to population growth, agricultural practices, and inadequate infrastructure.

- Cybersecurity is a major concern for businesses and governments alike, as cyber attacks can result in significant financial losses, damage to critical infrastructure, and breaches of sensitive information.

- The increasing prevalence of mental health issues among young people is a major concern, necessitating the implementation of preventative measures and improved access to mental health services.

6.

To carefully think about or include something when making a decision or forming an opinion.

To take into consideration

- When crafting public health policies, it is vital to take into consideration the diverse needs of various population groups, including age, socio-economic status, and cultural background.

- Urban planners need to take into consideration the impact of climate change on infrastructure and design more resilient and sustainable cities.

- The jury must take into consideration all relevant evidence before making a decision in a court case to ensure a fair and just outcome.

7.

To improve one's knowledge or comprehension of a subject or situation.

To gain a better understanding

- Researchers continue to study the human brain to gain a better understanding of neurological disorders, which could potentially lead to improved treatment methods.

- To gain a better understanding of the historical context, students should examine primary sources alongside secondary literature.

- By analyzing consumer behavior, marketers can gain a better understanding of their target audience and develop more effective advertising strategies.

8.

A major or important effect on something.

A significant impact

- The introduction of the internet has had a significant impact on the way people communicate, access information, and conduct business.

- Climate change has a significant impact on agriculture, with rising temperatures and shifting precipitation patterns affecting crop yields and food security.

- Public transportation infrastructure plays a significant role in reducing traffic congestion and air pollution, leading to a healthier and more sustainable urban environment.

9.

To be greatly influenced or harmed by something.

Severely affected by

- Coastal communities are often severely affected by natural disasters, such as hurricanes and tsunamis, due to their proximity to the ocean and low-lying terrain.

- Developing countries are typically more severely affected by the consequences of climate change, as they lack the resources and infrastructure to adapt effectively.

- The global economy was severely affected by the COVID-19 pandemic, with businesses closing down and unemployment rates skyrocketing.

10.

The underlying or primary reason for a problem or issue.

The root cause of

- Poverty is often considered the root cause of many social issues, including crime, drug addiction, and poor educational outcomes.

- A lack of access to clean water and sanitation facilities is the root cause of many health problems in developing nations, leading to the spread of waterborne diseases.

- Miscommunication and misunderstandings are frequently the root cause of conflicts, emphasizing the importance of effective communication skills in both personal and professional settings.

11.

To focus attention or raise awareness about a specific issue or topic.

To draw attention to

- The documentary aims to draw attention to the devastating effects of plastic pollution on marine life and encourage people to reduce their plastic consumption.

- Activists have been successful in drawing attention to the issue of income inequality and its negative consequences on society as a whole.

- Scientists have been trying to draw attention to the alarming rate of deforestation and its impact on biodiversity, urging governments to implement stronger conservation measures.

12.

To devise or propose a plan to solve a problem.

To come up with a solution

- Policymakers must work collaboratively with experts from various fields to come up with a solution to the growing problem of air pollution in urban areas.

- Engineers and architects are constantly challenged to come up with innovative solutions to address the increasing demand for sustainable and energy-efficient buildings.

- The international community must unite to come up with a solution to the global refugee crisis, providing support and resources for those displaced by conflict and persecution.

13.

To establish or enforce more rigorous rules or restrictions.

To impose stricter regulations

- In an effort to combat climate change, many countries have opted to impose stricter regulations on greenhouse gas emissions from industrial and transportation sectors.

- To ensure food safety, governments must impose stricter regulations on food production, handling, and distribution processes.

- The authorities should impose stricter regulations on the disposal of hazardous waste to prevent contamination of soil and water sources.

14.

To stimulate or increase economic development.

To boost economic growth

- Investing in education and infrastructure can significantly boost economic growth, as it creates a skilled workforce and facilitates the movement of goods and services.

- Lowering trade barriers and encouraging international cooperation can boost economic growth by providing access to new markets and fostering innovation.

- The development of small and medium-sized enterprises (SMEs) plays a crucial role in boosting economic growth, as they generate employment opportunities and contribute to local economies.

15.

To inform or educate people about a particular issue or concern.

To raise awareness of

- Environmental organizations often use social media campaigns to raise awareness of endangered species and the importance of conservation efforts.

- Community-based initiatives can be effective in raising awareness of mental health issues and reducing the stigma associated with seeking help.

- Educators should incorporate lessons on digital citizenship into their curricula to raise awareness of online safety and the responsible use of technology.

16.

To add to or exacerbate an existing issue.

To contribute to the problem

- The overuse of antibiotics in both human medicine and agriculture is known to contribute to the problem of antibiotic resistance, making it more difficult to treat bacterial infections.

- Deforestation and the burning of fossil fuels contribute significantly to the problem of climate change, as they release large amounts of carbon dioxide into the atmosphere.

- Unhealthy lifestyle choices, such as poor diet and lack of exercise, contribute to the problem of obesity, increasing the risk of various health complications.

17.

To find a compromise or equilibrium between competing factors or interests.

To strike a balance

- Educators must strike a balance between teaching fundamental knowledge and fostering creativity to ensure students develop well-rounded skill sets for the future.

- Urban planners should strike a balance between preserving green spaces and accommodating the growing population in cities, creating sustainable living environments.

- It is important for individuals to strike a balance between work and personal life, as neglecting either aspect can lead to stress and burnout.

18.

A thorough and complete strategy that addresses all aspects of a problem or situation.

A comprehensive approach

- A comprehensive approach to tackling climate change would involve reducing greenhouse gas emissions, promoting renewable energy, and protecting natural ecosystems.

- Addressing the issue of poverty requires a comprehensive approach that includes improving access to education, healthcare, and economic opportunities.

- To combat the global drug crisis, a comprehensive approach that includes prevention, treatment, and law enforcement efforts is necessary.

19.

The lasting effects or results of an action or decision.

Long-term consequences

- The long-term consequences of air pollution include an increased risk of respiratory diseases, reduced life expectancy, and damage to ecosystems.

- Failing to address the growing problem of plastic pollution can have long-term consequences for marine life and the overall health of our oceans.

- The long-term consequences of deforestation include loss of biodiversity, disruption of local communities, and contribution to climate change.

20.

A large number or wide variety of choices or alternatives.

A plethora of options

- With a plethora of options available for online learning, students can now access educational resources from virtually anywhere in the world.

- Consumers today are faced with a plethora of options when it comes to choosing sustainable products, making it easier to adopt environmentally friendly practices.

- Modern technology offers a plethora of options for communication, allowing people to stay connected with friends, family, and colleagues across the globe.

21.

To accomplish a desired outcome or goal.

To achieve success

- To achieve success in the competitive job market, graduates should focus on developing both technical skills and soft skills, such as communication and problem-solving abilities.

- Athletes must maintain a strict training regimen, balanced diet, and positive mindset to achieve success in their chosen sport.

- In order to achieve success in implementing new policies, governments should involve all relevant stakeholders, establish clear objectives, and allocate sufficient resources.

22.

To close the distance or differences between two things or groups.

To bridge the gap

- Educational programs and scholarships aimed at underprivileged students can help bridge the gap in educational opportunities and promote social mobility.

- Digital literacy initiatives can help bridge the gap between those who have access to technology and information and those who do not, reducing the digital divide.

- Cross-cultural exchange programs can bridge the gap between different cultures, fostering understanding and respect among diverse populations.

23.

change in the primary area of attention or concern.

A shift in focus

- A shift in focus from fossil fuels to renewable energy sources, such as solar and wind power, is necessary for mitigating the effects of climate change.

- To address rising obesity rates, there should be a shift in focus from solely treating the condition to emphasizing prevention through education on healthy lifestyles.

- A shift in focus from quantity to quality of economic growth could lead to more sustainable development, prioritizing well-being and the environment over mere GDP growth.

24.

To encourage or support joint efforts or teamwork.

To foster collaboration

- Interdisciplinary research projects can foster collaboration among experts from various fields, leading to innovative solutions to complex problems.

- International agreements and partnerships are essential to foster collaboration on global issues, such as climate change, poverty, and human rights.

- Creating an inclusive and supportive work environment can foster collaboration among employees, improving productivity and overall job satisfaction.

25.

A group of employees or laborers with advanced abilities or expertise.

Highly skilled workforce

- A highly skilled workforce is vital for maintaining a competitive edge in the global economy, as it drives innovation and attracts investment.

- Countries with a highly skilled workforce often experience higher levels of economic growth and enjoy better living standards.

- Investing in education and vocational training programs is essential for developing a highly skilled workforce that can adapt to the rapidly changing job market.

26.

To confront or deal with difficulties or obstacles.

To face challenges

- As the world becomes more interconnected, nations must face challenges such as cybersecurity threats, global pandemics, and economic instability, requiring coordinated international efforts.

- Students entering the workforce must be prepared to face challenges associated with technological advancements and the evolving job market, necessitating lifelong learning and adaptability.

- Environmental conservationists face challenges in balancing the need for economic development with the preservation of natural habitats and resources, highlighting the importance of sustainable practices.

27.

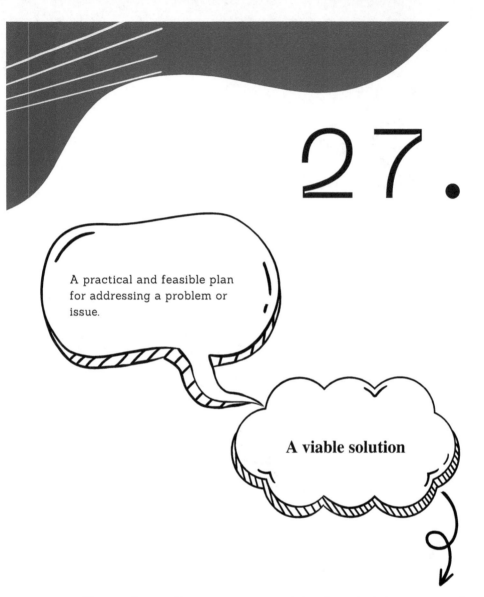

A practical and feasible plan for addressing a problem or issue.

A viable solution

- The use of renewable energy sources, such as solar and wind power, presents a viable solution to reducing our dependence on fossil fuels and addressing climate change.

- Telecommuting has emerged as a viable solution for reducing traffic congestion and improving work-life balance, particularly in the wake of the COVID-19 pandemic.

- Investing in public transportation infrastructure, such as efficient mass transit systems, is a viable solution for mitigating urban air pollution and decreasing greenhouse gas emissions.

28.

Unavoidable results or outcomes that follow a specific action or event.

Inevitable consequences

- The rapid depletion of natural resources, such as clean water and fertile soil, can have inevitable consequences on global food security and the livelihoods of local communities.

- The continued reliance on fossil fuels for energy production has inevitable consequences for the environment, including air pollution and climate change.

- Urbanization and population growth can lead to inevitable consequences, such as increased pressure on infrastructure and public services, necessitating sustainable planning and development strategies.

29.

To encourage or support fairness and equal treatment for all.

To promote equality

- Implementing progressive tax systems and providing robust social safety nets can help promote equality by reducing income disparities and supporting vulnerable populations.

- Ensuring equal access to education and healthcare for all citizens is essential to promote equality and foster social cohesion.

- Encouraging diversity and inclusion in the workplace can promote equality by creating a level playing field for all employees, regardless of their background or circumstances.

30.

The deterioration or damage to the natural environment caused by human activity or other factors.

Environmental degradation

- The indiscriminate use of pesticides in agriculture contributes to environmental degradation, contaminating soil and water sources, and harming ecosystems.

- Deforestation and habitat destruction are significant drivers of environmental degradation, leading to the loss of biodiversity and disruption of natural processes.

- Unsustainable industrial practices and waste disposal methods can cause environmental degradation, impacting air and water quality, and ultimately human health.

31.

In a period of time that can be reasonably predicted or anticipated.

In the foreseeable future

- In the foreseeable future, artificial intelligence and automation are expected to transform various industries, requiring workers to adapt and acquire new skills.

- Due to rapid technological advancements, it is likely that renewable energy sources will become even more accessible and cost-effective in the foreseeable future.

- With the ongoing effects of climate change, more frequent and severe weather events are anticipated in the foreseeable future, underscoring the need for effective disaster preparedness and mitigation strategies.

32.

A significant or sudden rise in quantity or level.

A dramatic increase

- The widespread adoption of smartphones and social media has led to a dramatic increase in the amount of time people spend online, impacting their daily lives and habits.

- Over the past few decades, there has been a dramatic increase in global tourism, bringing both economic benefits and challenges to popular destinations.

- As a result of climate change and habitat loss, many species have experienced a dramatic increase in their vulnerability to extinction, raising concerns about the future of biodiversity.

33.

To utilize or take advantage of the available resources or opportunities.

To harness the potential

- To harness the potential of renewable energy, governments should invest in research and development, as well as create incentives for businesses and individuals to adopt clean technologies.

- Educational institutions must adapt their curricula and teaching methods to harness the potential of digital technologies, providing students with the skills needed to thrive in the modern world.

- Collaborative efforts between public and private sectors can harness the potential of innovative solutions to address pressing societal issues, such as poverty, healthcare, and environmental sustainability.

44.

To adjust or modify one's behavior or approach in response to new circumstances or conditions.

To adapt to changes

- Businesses must continually innovate and adapt to changes in consumer preferences, market conditions, and technological advancements to remain competitive.

- As the effects of climate change become more pronounced, communities must adapt to changes in weather patterns, sea levels, and resource availability to ensure their long-term resilience.

- In an increasingly globalized world, individuals must be prepared to adapt to changes in the job market, cultural dynamics, and technological landscape to succeed personally and professionally.

35.

An urgent or important problem that requires immediate attention.

A pressing issue

- Addressing climate change is a pressing issue that requires urgent action from governments, businesses, and individuals to mitigate its long-term impacts on the planet and future generations.

- The growing problem of income inequality has become a pressing issue in many countries, leading to social unrest and demands for more equitable economic policies.

- Ensuring access to clean water and sanitation for all is a pressing issue, particularly in developing nations where millions of people still lack these basic necessities.

36.

The most advanced, innovative, or state-of-the-art devices or systems.

Cutting-edge technology

- Researchers are increasingly relying on cutting-edge technology, such as CRISPR gene editing, to develop new treatments for genetic disorders and improve agricultural productivity.

- The automotive industry is embracing cutting-edge technology to develop electric and self-driving vehicles, which can potentially reduce emissions and improve traffic safety.

- In education, the implementation of cutting-edge technology, such as virtual reality and artificial intelligence, can enhance the learning experience and better prepare students for future careers.

37.

A consistent or gradual decrease in quantity or quality.

A steady decline

- Over the past century, there has been a steady decline in the use of coal as a primary energy source, due to the rise of cleaner alternatives and concerns about its environmental impact.

- Many developed countries have experienced a steady decline in birth rates, leading to concerns about aging populations and the future sustainability of social welfare systems.

- The steady decline in biodiversity, largely driven by human activities such as habitat destruction and overexploitation, has raised alarm among conservationists and policymakers.

38.

To enjoy or take advantage of the positive outcomes or advantages of a situation.

To reap the benefits

- In order to reap the benefits of globalization, countries must invest in education, infrastructure, and technological innovation to remain competitive in the global market.

- Embracing a healthy lifestyle, including a balanced diet and regular exercise, can help individuals reap the benefits of improved physical and mental well-being.

- Businesses that adopt sustainable practices and prioritize corporate social responsibility can reap the benefits of enhanced reputation, customer loyalty, and long-term profitability.

39.

To lessen or reduce the negative impacts or consequences of something.

To mitigate the effects

- Governments and organizations must implement measures to mitigate the effects of climate change, such as investing in renewable energy and promoting sustainable land-use practices.

- Developing coping strategies and support networks can help individuals mitigate the effects of stress and maintain their mental well-being in challenging circumstances.

- Infrastructure improvements, such as flood barriers and early warning systems, can help communities mitigate the effects of natural disasters and enhance their overall resilience.

40.

A deep, lasting, or significant influence on something.

A profound effect

- The advent of the internet has had a profound effect on virtually all aspects of modern life, from communication and commerce to education and entertainment.

- Early childhood experiences and education can have a profound effect on an individual's cognitive, social, and emotional development, shaping their future success and well-being.

- Government policies and regulations can have a profound effect on economic growth, social equality, and environmental sustainability, highlighting the importance of effective governance.

41.

The arrival or introduction of new technological innovations.

The advent of technology

- The advent of technology has revolutionized the way people communicate, making it easier to stay connected with friends and family across the globe.

- In the healthcare sector, the advent of technology has led to significant improvements in diagnostics, treatment options, and patient care, ultimately saving countless lives.

- The advent of technology has had a major impact on the job market, creating new opportunities while rendering some traditional professions obsolete.

42.

A widely-held but mistaken belief or idea.

A common misconception

- A common misconception is that sustainable practices are always more expensive, when in reality, they can often save money in the long run through reduced resource consumption and waste.

- It is a common misconception that low-fat diets are inherently healthy; however, not all fats are created equal, and some, like those found in avocados and nuts, are beneficial to our health.

- A common misconception about online privacy is that using incognito mode in a browser ensures complete anonymity, but this only prevents browsing history from being saved on the user's device.

43.

To make a problem or issue worse or more severe.

To exacerbate the problem

- The rapid urbanization of developing countries can exacerbate the problem of waste management, as infrastructure and resources often struggle to keep pace with the growing population.

- Relying on short-term solutions to address water scarcity, such as drilling deeper wells, can exacerbate the problem by depleting groundwater resources more quickly.

- Misinformation spread through social media can exacerbate the problem of vaccine hesitancy, leading to lower vaccination rates and increased risk of disease outbreaks.

44.

> To distribute or assign resources such as time, money, or personnel to various tasks or projects.

To allocate resources

- Governments must allocate resources effectively to ensure access to essential public services, such as healthcare, education, and infrastructure, for all citizens.

- Companies must carefully allocate resources to research and development, marketing, and employee training to stay competitive and foster innovation.

- Non-profit organizations need to allocate resources efficiently to maximize their impact and ensure that donations are directed towards their intended beneficiaries.

45.

To guarantee the long-term viability or endurance of a system or practice.

To ensure sustainability

- To ensure sustainability, businesses must adopt environmentally friendly practices, such as reducing waste, conserving energy, and using renewable resources.

- Governments can implement policies and regulations to ensure sustainability in urban planning, such as promoting public transportation, green spaces, and energy-efficient buildings.

- Agriculture practices, like crop rotation and organic farming, can help ensure sustainability by preserving soil fertility, reducing chemical pollution, and maintaining biodiversity.

46.

To improve or increase the effectiveness or efficiency of an action or process.

To enhance performance

- Companies can invest in employee training and development programs to enhance performance and boost overall productivity.

- Athletes often incorporate strength training, conditioning exercises, and proper nutrition into their routines to enhance performance in their respective sports.

- Incorporating technology into the classroom, such as interactive whiteboards and online learning platforms, can help enhance performance by engaging students and personalizing instruction.

47.

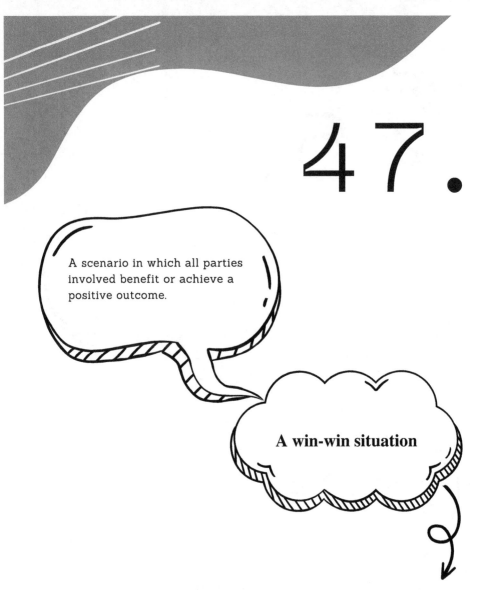

A scenario in which all parties involved benefit or achieve a positive outcome.

A win-win situation

- Implementing energy-efficient measures in buildings can create a win-win situation, as it reduces energy consumption and operating costs while also benefiting the environment.

- Encouraging telecommuting can be a win-win situation for employers and employees alike, as it may increase productivity and job satisfaction while reducing costs associated with office space and commuting.

- Establishing partnerships between businesses and non-profit organizations can create a win-win situation, as businesses improve their public image while non-profits gain access to resources and support.

48.

A large amount or abundance of useful knowledge or data.

A wealth of information

- The internet provides a wealth of information on nearly any topic, making it an invaluable resource for research, learning, and personal development.

- Libraries offer a wealth of information in the form of books, periodicals, and other resources, making them important community hubs for education and knowledge sharing.

- Attending conferences and seminars can expose attendees to a wealth of information from experts in their field, fostering professional growth and networking opportunities.

49.

To have more advantages or benefits compared to the disadvantages or negative aspects.

To outweigh the drawbacks

- While there are concerns about privacy and security in the digital age, the convenience and accessibility of online services often outweigh the drawbacks for many users.

- Although urban living can be associated with higher costs and environmental challenges, the availability of job opportunities, cultural experiences, and social connections often outweigh the drawbacks.

- The benefits of renewable energy sources, such as reduced greenhouse gas emissions and long-term cost savings, generally outweigh the drawbacks, such as the initial investment required for installation.

50.

To teach or encourage a feeling of obligation or duty in someone.

To instill a sense of responsibility

- Environmental education programs can instill a sense of responsibility in young people, encouraging them to adopt sustainable practices and become advocates for conservation.

- Volunteering and community service activities can help instill a sense of responsibility in individuals, fostering empathy, and commitment to social causes.

- Encouraging open communication, teamwork, and accountability in the workplace can instill a sense of responsibility among employees, leading to increased motivation and job satisfaction.

51.

A feeling of being accepted, valued, and connected within a group or community.

A sense of belonging

- Creating a welcoming and inclusive environment in schools and workplaces can foster a sense of belonging, contributing to improved mental health and overall well-being.

- Participating in clubs, social organizations, or community groups can provide individuals with a sense of belonging, helping them build connections and feel supported.

- Celebrating cultural diversity and encouraging the sharing of traditions can help promote a sense of belonging and acceptance among people from different backgrounds.

52.

To develop or nurture an optimistic outlook or approach to life.

To cultivate a positive attitude

- Encouraging mindfulness and self-reflection can help individuals cultivate a positive attitude, improving their ability to cope with stress and adversity.

- Teachers can cultivate a positive attitude in their students by fostering a growth mindset, celebrating achievements, and providing constructive feedback.

- Engaging in regular physical activity, maintaining a healthy diet, and getting adequate sleep can all contribute to cultivating a positive attitude and overall well-being.

53.

Closely connected or interdependent in a way that cannot be easily separated or disentangled.

Inextricably linked

- Economic development and environmental sustainability are inextricably linked, as responsible resource management and clean technologies are essential for long-term growth and prosperity.

- Mental and physical health are inextricably linked, with one often impacting the other, highlighting the importance of a holistic approach to wellness.

- Education and social mobility are inextricably linked, as access to quality education can provide individuals with the skills and opportunities needed to improve their circumstances.

54.

> To succeed or flourish in a setting characterized by rivalry or competition.

To thrive in a competitive environment

- To thrive in a competitive environment, businesses must continually innovate, adapt to changing market conditions, and focus on delivering exceptional customer experiences.

- Students who develop strong critical thinking, problem-solving, and communication skills are better equipped to thrive in a competitive environment, both academically and professionally.

- Embracing lifelong learning and staying current with industry trends can help professionals thrive in a competitive environment and advance their careers.

55.

A diverse and balanced educational experience that includes various subjects and disciplines.

A well-rounded education

- A well-rounded education includes not only core academic subjects but also exposure to the arts, physical education, and extracurricular activities that foster personal growth and social development.

- To provide a well-rounded education, schools should prioritize teaching essential life skills, such as financial literacy, digital competency, and emotional intelligence.

- A well-rounded education should also emphasize the development of critical thinking, creativity, and collaboration, preparing students for success in an increasingly complex and interconnected world.

56.

To experience a significant change or alteration in form, nature, or character.

To undergo a transformation

- The retail industry has undergone a significant transformation in recent years, with the rise of e-commerce and changing consumer preferences driving a shift towards online shopping and omnichannel experiences.

- Urban landscapes often undergo transformations as cities evolve, with revitalization projects and new infrastructure shaping the character and functionality of neighborhoods.

- As individuals progress through life, they may undergo transformations in their personal and professional identities, driven by experiences, relationships, and changing priorities.

57.

To interrupt or put an end to a repeating sequence of negative events or actions.

To break the vicious cycle

- To break the vicious cycle of poverty, policymakers must invest in education, healthcare, and social safety nets, empowering individuals to improve their circumstances and create better opportunities for future generations.

- Addressing mental health issues early and providing appropriate support can help break the vicious cycle of stress, depression, and anxiety that can negatively impact a person's well-being.

- Implementing sustainable resource management practices can help break the vicious cycle of overexploitation and environmental degradation, ensuring the long-term viability of ecosystems and the communities that depend on them.

58.

To clarify or reveal new information about a subject or issue.

To shed light on

- Scientific research has shed light on the mechanisms underlying many diseases, paving the way for the development of more targeted and effective treatments.

- The examination of historical documents and artifacts can shed light on the cultural, political, and economic factors that shaped societies in the past, providing valuable context for understanding the present.

- Analyzing data and trends can shed light on consumer behavior and preferences, helping businesses make more informed decisions about product development and marketing strategies.

59.

A wide variety or assortment of different elements or components.

A diverse array of

- Universities offer a diverse array of academic programs and extracurricular activities, allowing students to explore their interests and develop well-rounded skill sets.

- A healthy diet should include a diverse array of fruits, vegetables, lean proteins, whole grains, and healthy fats to ensure that all nutritional needs are met.

- Modern cities are characterized by a diverse array of architectural styles, public spaces, and cultural institutions, reflecting their dynamic histories and evolving identities.

60.

Something that has both positive and negative consequences or effects.

A double-edged sword

- Technology can be a double-edged sword, offering unprecedented opportunities for communication, innovation, and productivity while also raising concerns about privacy, security, and social isolation.

- Globalization is often seen as a double-edged sword, as it fosters economic growth and cultural exchange but can also exacerbate income inequality and environmental degradation.

- Flexibility in the workplace can be a double-edged sword, providing employees with greater autonomy and work-life balance but potentially leading to blurred boundaries and increased expectations for availability.

61.

To encourage or promote the development of new ideas, methods, or technologies.

To foster innovation

- Encouraging collaboration, open communication, and risk-taking within organizations can help foster innovation and drive growth.

- Governments can foster innovation by investing in research and development, supporting startups, and creating a favorable regulatory environment for new technologies and industries.

- Educational institutions can foster innovation by incorporating project-based learning, interdisciplinary studies, and opportunities for real-world problem-solving into their curricula.

62.

> Never-before-seen or unique chances or prospects for growth, development, or achievement.

Unprecedented opportunities

- The rapid pace of technological advancement has created unprecedented opportunities for individuals to access information, learn new skills, and connect with others around the world.

- Emerging markets often present unprecedented opportunities for businesses to expand their reach, tap into new consumer bases, and diversify their operations.

- Addressing global challenges such as climate change, inequality, and resource scarcity requires creative solutions and offers unprecedented opportunities for innovation and collaboration across sectors and disciplines.

63.

A straightforward, unambiguous, and effective plan or method for addressing a problem or issue.

A clear-cut solution

- Addressing climate change is a complex issue without a clear-cut solution, requiring the cooperation of governments, businesses, and individuals to implement a variety of mitigation and adaptation strategies.

- The debate over the optimal balance between privacy and security in the digital age has no clear-cut solution, as different stakeholders prioritize different values and interests.

- Reducing income inequality is a multifaceted challenge without a clear-cut solution, necessitating a combination of policy interventions, educational initiatives, and private sector commitments to promote equitable growth.

64.

To create the conditions or context in which a specific event or development can occur.

To set the stage for

- Early childhood education sets the stage for a child's academic success by providing a strong foundation in literacy, numeracy, and social-emotional development.

- Implementing strong environmental regulations can set the stage for sustainable growth, encouraging businesses to adopt cleaner technologies and practices.

- Investing in public infrastructure, such as transportation, sanitation, and energy systems, sets the stage for improved quality of life, economic development, and social mobility.

65.

To make it possible or easier for something to happen or develop by removing obstacles or providing necessary resources.

To pave the way for

- Scientific breakthroughs in fields such as genetics, artificial intelligence, and renewable energy pave the way for new technologies and applications that can transform industries and improve lives.

- International agreements and treaties, such as the Paris Agreement on climate change, can pave the way for coordinated global action to address pressing challenges.

- Fostering a culture of inclusivity and diversity in the workplace can pave the way for improved collaboration, innovation, and employee satisfaction.

66.

To be very close to or on the brink of experiencing a particular event, change, or situation.

To be on the verge of

- Researchers are on the verge of discovering new treatments for certain diseases, thanks to advancements in genetic engineering and personalized medicine.

- Some coastal cities are on the verge of experiencing severe flooding due to rising sea levels caused by climate change, necessitating urgent adaptation measures.

- With rapid technological advancements and the rise of automation, many industries are on the verge of significant transformations, requiring businesses and workers to adapt to new realities.

67.

To be proactive or take the first step in starting or leading a project, action, or movement.

To take the initiative

- Employees who take the initiative to identify and solve problems, improve processes, or develop new ideas are often seen as valuable assets in the workplace.

- Governments can take the initiative to address environmental challenges by implementing policies that encourage the adoption of sustainable practices and the development of clean technologies.

- Educators can take the initiative to create inclusive learning environments by adapting their teaching methods to accommodate diverse learning styles and needs.

68.

An issue or concern of the highest priority or significance.

A matter of utmost importance

- Ensuring access to quality education for all is a matter of utmost importance, as it contributes to social mobility, economic development, and global progress.

- Addressing the impacts of climate change and promoting environmental sustainability is a matter of utmost importance for the well-being of both current and future generations.

- Preserving cultural heritage and promoting intercultural understanding is a matter of utmost importance, as it fosters social cohesion and helps build inclusive societies.

69.

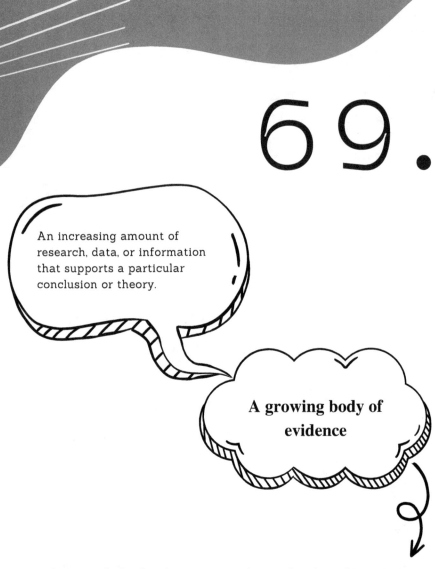

An increasing amount of research, data, or information that supports a particular conclusion or theory.

A growing body of evidence

- A growing body of evidence suggests that regular physical activity, a balanced diet, and sufficient sleep are crucial components of overall health and well-being.

- There is a growing body of evidence highlighting the benefits of early intervention and support for children with developmental delays or disabilities.

- A growing body of evidence indicates that diverse and inclusive workforces can lead to improved decision-making, innovation, and financial performance.

70.

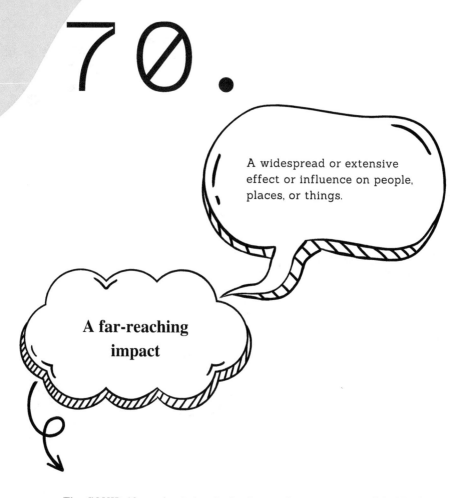

A widespread or extensive effect or influence on people, places, or things.

A far-reaching impact

- The COVID-19 pandemic has had a far-reaching impact on global health, economies, and social structures, prompting a reevaluation of priorities and systems.

- Technological innovations, such as the internet and smartphones, have had far-reaching impacts on how we communicate, work, and access information.

- Climate change has far-reaching impacts on ecosystems, agriculture, and human settlements, necessitating urgent action to mitigate and adapt to its effects.

71.

A difficult or intimidating task or problem that requires significant effort or resources to overcome.

A daunting challenge

- Addressing global issues such as climate change, poverty, and inequality presents a daunting challenge that requires collaboration and innovation across sectors and nations.

- Adapting to the rapidly changing job market and staying competitive in the face of automation and technological advancements can be a daunting challenge for both workers and businesses.

- Ensuring food security and sustainable agricultural practices for a growing global population is a daunting challenge that necessitates innovative solutions and responsible resource management.

72.

To take advantage of or make the most of favorable situations or circumstances.

To capitalize on opportunities

- To capitalize on opportunities in emerging markets, businesses must conduct thorough market research, understand local cultures and regulations, and develop tailored strategies.

- Students can capitalize on opportunities for personal and professional growth by participating in internships, extracurricular activities, and networking events.

- Policymakers can capitalize on opportunities to promote sustainable development by investing in clean energy, green infrastructure, and innovative technologies.

73.

A noticeable or significant enhancement or betterment in quality, performance, or results.

A marked improvement

- Implementing evidence-based teaching strategies and providing targeted support can lead to a marked improvement in student outcomes and achievement.

- A marked improvement in air and water quality can be observed when industries adopt cleaner technologies and governments enforce strict environmental regulations.

- Investing in public health initiatives, such as vaccination campaigns and preventative care, can result in a marked improvement in overall population health and well-being.

74.

To present or create a potential danger or risk to someone or something.

To pose a threat

- The loss of biodiversity and habitat destruction pose a threat to the health of ecosystems and the many services they provide, including food production, water purification, and climate regulation.

- Cybersecurity breaches and data theft pose a threat to individuals, businesses, and governments, highlighting the need for robust security measures and increased vigilance.

- The spread of misinformation and the proliferation of fake news pose a threat to democratic processes and social cohesion, necessitating efforts to promote media literacy and fact-checking.

75.

To accept, value, and celebrate differences among people, cultures, or ideas.

To embrace diversity

- To embrace diversity, organizations must foster inclusive cultures, implement equitable policies, and promote representation at all levels of decision-making.

- Educational institutions can embrace diversity by providing culturally responsive curricula, supporting students from diverse backgrounds, and promoting tolerance and understanding.

- Embracing diversity in our personal lives, through our relationships and experiences, can enrich our perspectives and contribute to a more empathetic and inclusive society.

76.

A sudden or rapid increase in the need or desire for a product, service, or resource.

A surge in demand

- The rapid growth of the middle class in emerging economies has led to a surge in demand for consumer goods, presenting opportunities and challenges for global businesses.

- A surge in demand for renewable energy sources, driven by concerns about climate change and energy security, has spurred innovation and investment in clean technologies.

- The COVID-19 pandemic created a surge in demand for remote work technologies and tools, prompting companies to quickly adapt and develop new solutions to support a distributed workforce.

77.

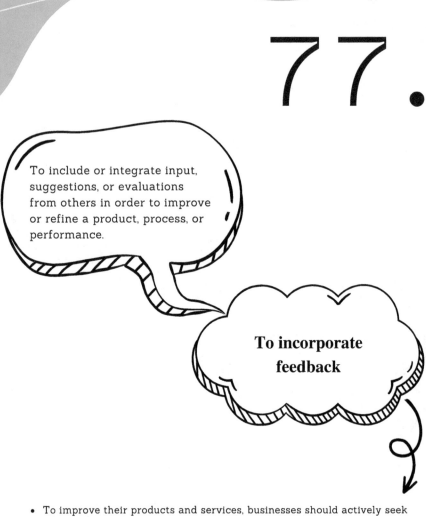

To include or integrate input, suggestions, or evaluations from others in order to improve or refine a product, process, or performance.

To incorporate feedback

- To improve their products and services, businesses should actively seek customer feedback and incorporate it into their decision-making and development processes.

- Teachers can enhance their teaching practices by incorporating feedback from students, colleagues, and professional development opportunities.

- To grow personally and professionally, individuals should be open to incorporating feedback from peers, mentors, and supervisors, using it as a valuable tool for self-improvement.

78.

To make the exchange of information, ideas, or feelings easier or more efficient between individuals or groups.

To facilitate communication

- Companies can use collaboration tools and platforms, such as video conferencing and project management software, to facilitate communication among remote or distributed teams.

- Governments can facilitate communication with citizens by providing accessible and transparent information through websites, social media, and public consultations.

- Educators can facilitate communication and collaboration among students by incorporating group projects, peer feedback, and interactive discussions into their teaching methods.

79.

To put new policies, procedures, or ideas into effect with the aim of improving a situation or achieving a goal.

To implement changes

- In order to enhance the educational system, it is vital for policymakers to implement changes that foster creativity and critical thinking.

- The government needs to implement changes in the healthcare sector to ensure that everyone has access to affordable, quality care.

- Implementing changes in the way we approach waste management can lead to a cleaner, more sustainable environment for future generations.

80.

A state of equilibrium or stability that is sensitive and easily disrupted, often referring to the need for careful management of competing interests or priorities.

A delicate balance

- Achieving a delicate balance between economic growth and environmental preservation is crucial for sustainable development.

- A delicate balance must be struck between preserving cultural heritage and embracing modernization in urban planning.

- Public health initiatives must maintain a delicate balance between individual rights and the overall wellbeing of the community.

81.

A passionate or intense discussion or argument involving strong disagreement or differing opinions.

A heated debate

- The heated debate surrounding immigration policies has divided public opinion and highlighted the need for a more inclusive approach.

- Gun control remains a heated debate in many countries, with advocates on both sides presenting compelling arguments.

- The role of technology in the classroom has sparked a heated debate among educators, parents, and students alike.

82.

A considerable, significant, or large quantity of something.

A substantial amount

- A substantial amount of research has been conducted on the impact of social media on mental health, yielding mixed results.

- The government has invested a substantial amount of resources in developing renewable energy sources to reduce carbon emissions.

- It is necessary to allocate a substantial amount of funding to address the rising problem of homelessness in urban areas.

83.

To take action against or fight the adverse effects of climate change, often through reducing greenhouse gas emissions and promoting sustainable practices.

To combat climate change

- To combat climate change, world leaders must work together to reduce greenhouse gas emissions and promote renewable energy sources.

- Reforestation and afforestation projects are essential tools to combat climate change by absorbing carbon dioxide from the atmosphere.

- Encouraging public transportation and the use of electric vehicles can help combat climate change by reducing our reliance on fossil fuels.

84.

A close relationship or connection between two variables or factors, suggesting that one may be directly or indirectly influencing the other.

A strong correlation

- A strong correlation exists between a country's investment in education and its overall economic growth.

- Studies have shown a strong correlation between regular exercise and improved mental health.

- There is a strong correlation between parental involvement in a child's education and the child's academic success.

85.

To nurture, promote, or encourage feelings of belonging, connectedness, and shared identity among a group of people.

To foster a sense of community

- Community events and gatherings can help foster a sense of community, promoting social cohesion and reducing feelings of isolation.

- Inclusive urban planning that encourages interaction among residents can foster a sense of community in growing cities.

- Schools can foster a sense of community by organizing extracurricular activities and encouraging parental engagement.

86.

A critical or decisive point in time or an event that has a significant impact on the course of a situation or development.

A pivotal moment

- The signing of the Paris Agreement was a pivotal moment in the global effort to address climate change.

- The discovery of penicillin marked a pivotal moment in the history of medicine, revolutionizing the treatment of bacterial infections.

- The fall of the Berlin Wall in 1989 was a pivotal moment in world history, symbolizing the end of the Cold War.

87.

To strengthen or increase backing, encouragement, or approval for an idea, cause, or person.

To bolster support

- The government should invest in public awareness campaigns to bolster support for environmental conservation initiatives.

- In order to bolster support for the new policy, the administration must effectively communicate its benefits to the public.

- The opposition party launched a series of rallies to bolster support ahead of the upcoming election.

88.

> A strong, reliable, or stable basis upon which something is built or established, often referring to principles, knowledge, or skills.

A solid foundation

- A solid foundation in reading and writing skills is essential for a child's academic success and future career prospects.

- Infrastructure development is key to providing a solid foundation for economic growth and prosperity.

- Establishing a solid foundation of trust and mutual understanding is crucial for successful diplomatic relations between nations.

89.

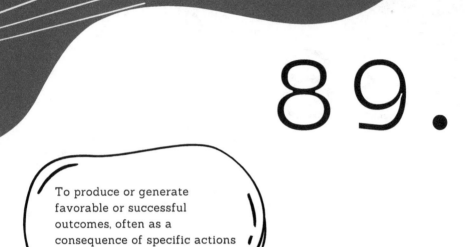

To produce or generate favorable or successful outcomes, often as a consequence of specific actions or efforts.

To yield positive results

- Investing in early childhood education has been shown to yield positive results in terms of cognitive development and long-term academic achievement.

- Implementing preventive health measures has been proven to yield positive results in reducing the incidence of chronic diseases.

- Companies that prioritize employee wellbeing and job satisfaction tend to yield positive results in terms of productivity and staff retention.

90.

A distinctive or remarkable instance that does not conform to a general rule or pattern.

A notable exception

- While most countries have experienced economic growth in recent years, the small island nation has been a notable exception, suffering from a recession.

- While fast food is generally considered unhealthy, some restaurant chains have made a notable exception by offering nutritious and wholesome options.

- Despite the trend towards digital communication, the resurgence of printed books in certain markets serves as a notable exception.

91.

An essential, necessary, or fundamental component or element of a larger whole.

An integral part

- Collaboration and teamwork are an integral part of a successful work environment, fostering innovation and productivity.

- Physical activity is an integral part of maintaining a healthy lifestyle, promoting overall wellbeing and reducing the risk of chronic diseases.

- Preserving cultural heritage is an integral part of maintaining a diverse and inclusive society.

92.

To promote or support behaviors or practices that contribute to physical, mental, or emotional wellbeing.

To encourage healthy habits

- Schools should implement nutrition education programs to encourage healthy habits in children from a young age.

- Public health campaigns can be effective in encouraging healthy habits, such as regular exercise and smoking cessation.

- Workplaces can encourage healthy habits by offering wellness programs and providing access to healthier food options in cafeterias.

93.

To manage, handle, or deal with mental or emotional strain or tension in a healthy and adaptive manner.

To cope with stress

- Engaging in regular exercise and mindfulness practices can help individuals cope with stress and improve their mental wellbeing.

- Building a strong support network is essential for individuals to cope with stress during challenging times.

- Time management and organizational skills can help students cope with stress related to academic workload and deadlines.

94.

> A labor force composed of individuals with varying backgrounds, experiences, and perspectives, often in terms of ethnicity, gender, age, or ability.

A diverse workforce

- A diverse workforce fosters creativity and innovation by bringing together individuals with unique perspectives and experiences.

- Companies that embrace a diverse workforce are more likely to attract and retain top talent from various backgrounds.

- To create a diverse workforce, organizations should implement inclusive hiring practices and promote a culture of respect and acceptance.

95.

A feasible, practical, or workable option or solution that can serve as an effective substitute or replacement for an existing one.

A viable alternative

- Renewable energy sources, such as solar and wind power, provide a viable alternative to fossil fuels, reducing greenhouse gas emissions.

- Online learning has become a viable alternative to traditional classroom education, offering flexibility and accessibility to learners around the world.

- Plant-based meat substitutes are emerging as a viable alternative for consumers seeking to reduce their meat consumption for health or environmental reasons.

96.

To create or develop a relationship of mutual understanding, trust, or sympathy, often in a social or professional context.

To establish a rapport

- Teachers should make an effort to establish a rapport with their students to create a positive and supportive learning environment.

- In negotiations, diplomats must establish a rapport with their counterparts to foster trust and facilitate productive discussions.

- Sales professionals often rely on their ability to establish a rapport with clients to build long-lasting business relationships.

97.

A wide range or variety of items, ideas, or elements that span a diverse set of categories or criteria.

A broad spectrum

- The new policy aims to address a broad spectrum of social issues, including poverty, education, and healthcare.

- The conference will bring together experts from a broad spectrum of disciplines to discuss solutions to pressing global challenges.

- The curriculum should cover a broad spectrum of subjects to provide students with a well-rounded education.

98.

A deep, significant, or lasting effect or influence on a person, situation, or environment.

A profound impact

- Climate change has a profound impact on ecosystems and biodiversity, leading to the extinction of many species.

- Technological advancements, such as the internet and smartphones, have had a profound impact on the way we live, work, and communicate.

- Socioeconomic factors, such as income and education, can have a profound impact on an individual's health outcomes and life expectancy.

99.

To maintain, reinforce, or contribute to the persistence of oversimplified or generalized beliefs or assumptions about a particular group or category of people.

To perpetuate stereotypes

- Media portrayals that rely on outdated and harmful cliches can serve to perpetuate stereotypes and reinforce prejudice.

- Education systems must challenge and dismantle biased curricula that perpetuate stereotypes and perpetuate inequality.

- Society must recognize and address the ways in which language and behavior can perpetuate stereotypes and contribute to discrimination.

100.

A situation in which everyone has an equal opportunity to succeed or compete fairly, without any unfair advantages or disadvantages.

A level playing field

- Ensuring a level playing field in education is essential for promoting social mobility and reducing inequality.

- Governments must implement policies that create a level playing field for small businesses to compete with large corporations.

- In sports, implementing rules and regulations that promote fair competition can create a level playing field for all athletes regardless of their background or socioeconomic status.

Final Words

Mastering the use of high-scoring collocations in your IELTS Writing Task 2 essay can greatly enhance your writing quality and help you achieve a higher band score.

By familiarizing yourself with these top 100 collocations, you'll be better equipped to express your ideas clearly and effectively. Remember, practice makes perfect – so, try incorporating these collocations in your practice essays and watch your writing skills soar!

Good luck on your IELTS journey, and may your hard work be rewarded with the score you desire.

READ MORE

TheBrainstormingStation.com